NO NEGATIVES

A Guide To Leadership
For Young People

Featuring:

Self-Esteem
Motivation
Communication
Career Development
Health
Literacy
Time Management
Community Service
Mentoring

J. Victor McGuire, Ph.D.
Colorado State University

McGraw-Hill, Inc.
College Custom Series

*New York   St. Louis   San Francisco   Auckland   Bogotá
Caracas   Hamburg   Lisbon   London   Madrid   Mexico   Milan   Montreal
New Delhi   Paris   San Juan   São Paulo   Singapore   Sydney   Tokyo   Toronto*

NO NEGATIVES
A Guide To Leadership For Young People

Copyright © 1992 by McGraw-Hill, Inc. All rights reserved. Printed in the United States of America. Except as permitted under the United States Copyright Act of 1976, no part of this publication may be reproduced or distributed in any form or by any means, or stored in a data base retrieval system, without prior written permission of the publisher.

Library of Congress Cataloging in Publication Data
Library of Congress Catalog Card Number 89-91959

McGuire, J. Victor
No Negatives

1 2 3 4 5 6 7 8 9 0 MALMAL 9 0 9 8 7 6 5 4 3 2

ISBN 07-045134-6

Editor: Jon K. Earl

Cover Design: Robert Howard

Printer/Binder: Malloy Lithographing, Inc.

ACKNOWLEDGEMENTS

Over the course of several years, a variety of people have supported and acknowledged the work I do. For this, I thank you all!

Mr. Louis McGuire
Ms. Ellen McGuire
Dr. Mack Clark
Mr. Wayne Parthun
Dr. Jane McDearmid
Dr. Tim Houlton
Dr. Rich Feller
Ms. Dee Wanger
Ms. Sally Hutchinson
Mr. Bill Grunewald
Ms. Margot Collins
Mr. Keith Babcock
Mr. Scott Babcock
Ms. Cindy Anderson
Dr. Eric Eversly
Ms. Kelly Stevens
Ms. Stacie Sakowski
Ms. Lisa Dillingham
Ms. Josette Dillman
Ms. Michele Compton
Ms. Julia Atwater
Ms. Kristen Svendsen
Ms. Jill Noel
Dr. Robert Williams
Ms. Julia K. McNamara
and all past, present & future ED255 students

HANKS

I hope everyone who reads this book will have a chance someday to meet its author, J. Victor McGuire. Victor is that special kind of person who immediately engages you, enjoys being with you, and makes you feel the world is a better place because you are a part of it.

This book will never replace an opportunity to meet Victor up close and personal, but it is a superb opportunity for every young person facing the challenges of growing up to experience Victor's beliefs about life, school, and young people. The book will take you through the steps necessary to confirm that you are a special person and that life is better when there are "no negatives." Victor is a master teacher, and this book is his masterpiece!

Victor believes that the most important ideas you have are those ideas you have about yourself. He knows the importance of school and the academic side of life, but he is committed to sharing with young people the strategies to help make you more effective human beings. Victor knows how important self esteem, motivation, communication and community involvement are to you and he has put together in this wonderful book a series of activities that will help you in each of these areas. This is not a "text book" in the usual sense, but in some ways it is a "course" in how to deal with the ups and downs, the joys and the disappointments, the challenges of growing up in a complex but exciting world.

The greatest thing about reading this book will be that you won't just be able to read it; you are going to want to go out and DO this book. It will help you to see the value in yourself and the people around you; it will help you feel better about the problems you face every day. In many ways it is likely to become a companion, a treasury of ideas to help you become all you are capable of becoming.

Victor often talks about life being a journey with you in the driver's seat. In this book he has provided a road map that will make the journey just a little more exciting, a little more rewarding, and a little more fun. I know you are going to like this book. It may be the most important book you ever read, but if it is not, at least you will have had an opportunity to spend time with the thoughts and suggestions of one of the most important young educators of our time, and then I hope you get to meet Victor some day in person. He will change your life. He has helped to change mine!

> Thomas R. Giblin
> Superintendent of Schools
> Guilford, Connecticut

These <u>Personal Points To Ponder</u> pages are provided at the end of each section of this book. Please use them to write down your thoughts, ideas and plans as you work through *No Negatives*.

TABLE OF CONTENTS

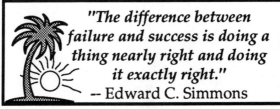

"The difference between failure and success is doing a thing nearly right and doing it exactly right."
-- Edward C. Simmons

INTRODUCTION

Hello, my name is J. Victor McGuire, the author of *No Negatives*. This book will be a little bit different than other books you have read. You see, this book is going to be a reader's participation book. You will not get away with just reading it and saying to yourself, "My what an interesting and thought-provoking book." With this book you will take an active role in experiencing the NO NEGATIVES CONCEPT, WHICH IS ACCEPTING AND APPRECIATING, NOT CRITICIZING AND COMPLAINING. Now if this concept is something you don't think you can buy into, fine. Simply put the book down and go about your business, or give it to someone who might utilize it to its fullest. Are you with me? If so, great. You are about to take part in quite the adventure.

Before we go on, you need to realize that you are the sole person responsible for making this book a success for you and the people around you. Once again, you are the main ingredient in this book. So, add some spice to your life and let's make it happen together!

Over the past few years I have been actively involved with an organization I founded, Spice of Life. Spice of Life's focus is on Self Esteem, Motivation, Communication and Community Involvement.

Through the course of *No Negatives* you will encounter testimonials from former Spice students that will reflect the spirit of *No Negatives*.

 "If we believed in walking down life's beaten path, we would seldom make any tracks of our own."
-- J. Victor McGuire

WHY SELF ESTEEM?

When you have positive self esteem, you look and feel good; you tend to be effective and productive in your daily life. Also, when you are feeling good about yourself you tend to give some of those traits away to other people, in a positive fashion.

Self esteem affects everyone we are around, especially our families. Can you imagine how harmonious your household would be if everyone felt confident and good about themselves? It can be contagious. Try it -- you will be amazed!

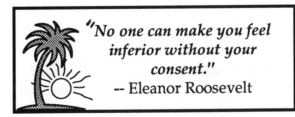

"No one can make you feel inferior without your consent."
-- Eleanor Roosevelt

SELF ESTEEM

No Negatives . . . what a title. Do you notice how the information we receive on a daily basis is generally negative? I do not want to give you a clouded view, so do something for me. Go get a newspaper and write down the titles of five stories on the first two pages.

1.

2.

3.

4.

5.

What did you find? If it was not mostly negative then you have found a newspaper that is the exception and not the rule. My guess is your paper talked about a few more negatives than positives. Why is that?

Here is an example you might be able to relate to. There is a fight at school. What happens? Everybody rushes over to check it out, right? Now, when somebody does something good how many of us rush over and watch?

Of course there are a lot of positive things going on in today's world, but unfortunately not enough of them are being recognized.

As you journey through this book, we will be exploring ways to better recognize and appreciate the positive things -- about ourselves and about others. Also, it is my hope that this will help you use your resources to become the best YOU you can be!

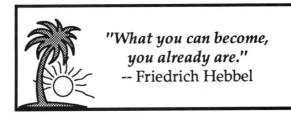

"What you can become, you already are."
-- Friedrich Hebbel

WHO ARE YOU

Earlier I introduced myself to you, so it is time you do the same.

Describe yourself in three words.

1.

2.

3.

Name five positive qualities about you.

1.

2.

3.

4.

5.

With this next section let's take a few minutes to evaluate who you are. Read through the following list of characteristics and rate yourself using the space provided below.

1=Never   2=Occasionally   3=Most of the time   4=Always

___ I feel secure about who I am.

___ I like other people's company.

___ I can make friends easily.

___ I feel important.

___ If I fail I try and try again.

___ I am honest in my feelings about other people.

___ I am good at helping other people.

___ I am special.

___ I can easily say "Thank You" after someone pays me a compliment.

___ I think of the idea first.

Getting to know yourself and learning to accept yourself for who and what you are is an essential step towards positive self esteem. Look at your list; go back through all the characteristics that you marked with a three or a four. These can be considered your strengths.

Ones or twos are characteristics you may want to improve upon. Appreciate your strengths, don't dwell on your weaknesses.

"Everybody has to be somebody to somebody to be anybody."
-- Malcolm S. Forbes

LEVELS OF SELF ESTEEM

(All Shapes & Sizes)

Now that you have established a better idea of who you are regarding self esteem, let us take a look at the different levels and begin to focus closer where you fit.

A. People having high levels of self esteem . . .

1. Feel self confident and believe in themselves.

2. Can take constructive criticism.

3. Are not threatened by failure.

4. Accept and appreciate situations, try not to criticize or complain.

5. Are most likely in good physical shape.

6. Are not critical of themselves to the point where they are constantly putting themselves down.

B. With an intermediate levels of self esteem you . . .

1. Are a cautious person.

2. Look for others to assist in your decision-making process.

3. Look for ways to please people.

Now, I realize this next level is of no real concern for you, but you may know someone on this level and may add some words of encouragement for them.

C. People experience low levels of self esteem generally possess these characteristics:

1. Loners.

2. Expect to fail.

3. Would rather isolate themselves from a group than participate.

4. Very sensitive to ridicule.

5. They find a way to fail rather than looking for ways to succeed.

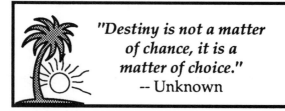

"Destiny is not a matter of chance, it is a matter of choice."
-- Unknown

**MOVE
ON**

Next is the process of how to implement or increase your positive self esteem. That can be achieved by working on your attitude. I realize we have all had some setbacks, but it is now time to make a fresh start and believe that you will only go up from here.

Before we continue with self esteem, let us consider how society looks at us. Unfortunately, if we look at ourselves too much we are viewed as being self-centered. So, before I ask you to take a look at yourself, I would like to share this story about a former seventh-grade class of mine.

Fashion Show 101

One day in class I happened to notice that one of my students was sporting some new clothes, so I made a comment that she looked good. Well, she did a double take and decided to become an instant fashion model. She started strutting her stuff, saying, "The pants are from The Limited, and the shoes are from Kinneys." Well, the whole class was cracking up! This particular student felt pretty good about herself, but she also had a great ability as a seventh grader to allow others to feel good about themselves. So I got to thinking about our impromptu fashion show. I wondered, "Wouldn't it be great if everyone modeled the clothes they wore to school!" So, the next day I asked "Who's next?" They all looked at me. It got very quiet. Then, at the back of the room a hand went up. A boy got out of his chair and began to recite, "The shoes are from Penneys, the pants are from The Gap..." It was great!

The entire class got into the spirit of it and paraded down our makeshift aisle, music and all.

No one cared about how they looked; it was just fun to show off a bit and not be judged by anyone. So, go ahead! Take a closer look. Have a fashion show in your head. Who cares?

> *"Some men see things as they are and say why? I dream of things that never were and say why not?"* -- George Bernard Shaw

STRENGTHS AND WEAKNESSES

If you are going to improve yourself, you should know your strengths and be able to build upon them.

In this exercise I want you to list your strengths and weaknesses.

Strengths	Weaknesses
1.	1.
2.	2.
3.	3.
4.	4.
5.	5.
6.	6.

Get with a close friend and discuss the positive nature of your strengths as well as some possible ways that you might work on reducing your weaknesses.

Now, if something is suggested that you don't like, but that you agree with, do not expend energy thinking about the fault -- instead use your energy to evaluate and possible remedy it.

"A great pleasure in life is doing what people say you cannot do."
-- Walter Gagehot

RISK TAKING

The next portion of self esteem deals with risk taking. Risk is a key factor in leadership. I want you and your friend to do something positive for someone else. Look how you can make their day!! Jot down your risk.

1. Together make a new friend.

2.

3.

4.

5.

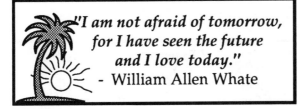

"I am not afraid of tomorrow, for I have seen the future and I love today."
- William Allen Whate

MAKING MISTAKES

From time to time as you go through life you will make mistakes. Some will be small, some big; some right, some wrong. But what is really important is how we choose to handle situations. We will never be perfect in life, and we must come to realize that mistakes are a part of everyday life. Do not believe your self-worth is gone when you make a mistake.

Strive for excellence -- punt the perfection. **Give yourself the right to be wrong!**

"Experience is not what happens to you; it is what you do with what happens to you." -- Aldous Huxley

CHRISTMAS EVERY DAY

At Home, School, Community

I am a firm believer in the notion that the more you do for others, the better you will you feel. A good example of this feeling is Christmas or Hannukkah, or any holiday where you give. The key to this is to give without expecting something in return. If you can do something for someone one day per week without expecting something in return, it has got to make you feel good. Let us start a good habit.

Here are some examples:

Parents: Okay, here you go -- let us start with the people who made it possible for us to be here. Do something for them that will just **freak them out!**

1. Clean the house.
2. Clean your room.
3. Make dinner.
4. Buy them a nice card.
5. Be nice to your brother or sister.

I will do the following:

1. I will . . .

2. I will . . .

3. I will . . .

After you finish with your parents, maybe you can blow some teacher's mind!

Teachers: As a classroom teacher I know what I would freak out about. The biggest hurdle for students is to understand that teachers are people too. They like compliments also.

Here are a few ideas:
1. Invite a teacher over for dinner.
2. Invite him or her to a movie with your friends.
3. If you enjoyed their class that day, tell them.

The main thing you might want to be concerned about is your motive. Remember, you are doing this for their sake, not yours. You are not expecting anything in return!

Finally, let us do something for the community. Occasionally around the holiday season you will see a story about a soup kitchen serving meals to needy families or homeless people seeking food, clothing, etc. I have taken students to the soup kitchen to work -- you got it right, work -- or better yet to give. So, get a few friends together, contact an area soup kitchen, and go and try to make some people's day a little brighter. Take some food, help prepare it, serve it, and then eat with them. Meet someone new. Do not judge them. Just accept and appreciate them for who they are. Some other examples would be to help at a senior citizens home or center for disadvantaged youth.

I realize that in order to do any of these things you will need to take some risks, and maybe for some of you it might be a lot of risks. Be prepared. Some people might not be appreciative -- that is okay. The key point is, how did YOU feel?

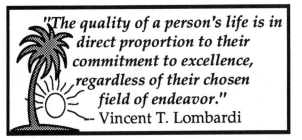

"The quality of a person's life is in direct proportion to their commitment to excellence, regardless of their chosen field of endeavor."
-- Vincent T. Lombardi

Now that you have spent time on your strengths and weaknesses, let's look at these a bit. Was it easier for you to put strengths or weaknesses down? My bet is that you spent more time on your weaknesses. If I am wrong, great; you have a good start towards this next section.

As I mentioned earlier, this is not going to be the type of book that will fill you with false hope about how you can do anything you choose -- let's get real! Basically that is a negative set up. You know why, don't you? If you set up unrealistic dreams that exceed your limitations, then you have set yourself up for failure. Psychologists have been quoted as saying that people seldom use more than 25 percent of their potential. That leaves 75 percent unused! Think of the possibilities. I wonder how much potential Einstein used? I wonder how much you use -- 2%? 7%? If I have said this once I have said it a thousand times: *"Spend positive time and positive energy on what you can accomplish, not on what you cannot."*

"Great minds have purposes, others have wishes."
-- Washington Irving

THE UP AND DOWN

I realize that occasionally we all play the comparison game. Either we do it consciously or unconsciously, but we do it. When someone passes us in the hall or on the street, we give them the old once-up-and-down look -- you know, starting from the shoes, we check them out all the way up to the head. The bad part is that we are setting ourselves for disappointment again, because if the person exceeds our expectation, if we feel they are similar or even better in some way, then there goes our self esteem. So the best way to avoid this is not to play the game.

Geneticists say that odds of our parents having another child like us are 1 in 102,000,000,000. We are not all the same, so let's face the fact that we are special and different. You are unique.

Well, there you have it. Before you go on to the next section, realize that you cannot be "self esteemed" in one setting or one reading. Go out and make it happen ... daily!

"Do not wait for your ship to come in, swim out to it."
-- Unknown

1. Feel good about how you perceive yourself. Accept yourself for who you are -- do not compare.
2. Do not take for granted your strengths and natural abilities. If you do something well, build on that strength.
3. Live for yourself so you can give yourself away to others occasionally.
4. Observe people you admire.
5. Believe in your potential and understand your limitations.

As you end each section, you will be provided with five pages to respond to five questions that relate to each area of focus. Please see these questions as a way to find out more about you. As you respond, allow yourself to take the path of growth. Obviously, there are not correct or incorrect answers, only honest and dishonest ones.

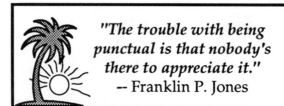

"The trouble with being punctual is that nobody's there to appreciate it."
-- Franklin P. Jones

1. I like myself most when I . . .

2. A perfect day for me would be . . .

"I believe in getting into hot water. I think it keeps you clean."
-- G.K. Chesterton

3. The last time I really made someone feel good was . . .

It made me feel . . . *(describe)*

4. The quality I wish I possessed . . *(tell why)*

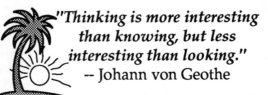

"Thinking is more interesting than knowing, but less interesting than looking."
-- Johann von Geothe

5. My positive habits are . . .

Before you go on to motivation, ask yourself the question, "Have I fully completed this section to the best of my ability?" If yes, proceed; if no, finish it!

When I was in "Spice of Life" I thought at the time that yeah, sure, this was great, and it's helping some now. But I am only going to feel this way while I am in the program. No way was it going to help me later on. But I was wrong. One of the things stressed in "Spice of Life" is self esteem, and one of the more important parts of self esteem is that in order to have a lot of it, you had to feel good about how you look, and overall feel good about yourself. I always thought, "Oh, I have no problem with that. I feel just fine about how I look, and I feel great about myself. Nobody else has hair like me or dresses like me. I am unique. I am original and different." And that's fine, looking different and original, but only to a certain extent. When you start looking too extreme, the atmosphere around you changes. People stare and yell rude things at you. Everything around you turns negative. If you know that, and what you are bringing on yourself, the stares, the negative comments, then that's fine ... as long as you can handle it.

But most of the time, even though you think it is not bothering you, it really is. When all those negative emotions and ugly stares are directed at you, YOU start feeling negatively, and your self esteem plunges. At that time you block the feelings, the true feelings, and replace them with anger. But the truth is it hurts, and it hurts BAD.

I did not know how bad I was feeling and how low my self

esteem was, until I changed my appearance when I moved. I was so tired of feeling so low and depressed, and most of all feeling so negatively all the time. When I changed th way I looked, I changed for the better, and for the first time I went into public with a new image.

I was not feeling defensive or self-conscious about the way I looked. I felt so good, and my self esteem was flying high! When I changed, the atmosphere around me changed. I was no longer the "center of attention," and instead of getting negative things directed at me I got compliments and positive remarks.

I felt so much better about myself. I felt so good about myself because I looked better. I no longer felt hesitant or uncomfortable when I went into malls or supermarkets by myself, because now I know if people are staring it is not because of how extreme and different I look, but because of how good I look -- and that feels GREAT.

Spice of Life did something so special and important for me. It helped me see the real world. It opened my eyes to see the truth. And the truth was that to survive out there you need all the positive self esteem you can muster. But when you are feeling so low about yourself because of the way you look, you have self esteem worth NOTHING. When you are feeling that bad about yourself you have to make some changes. Finally I saw that, and I am glad I did now rather than later in life.

Spice did that for me. It showed me that by looking your best and feeling your best and working up to your true potential, you feel so good it is hard to be in a bad mood, or to not be smiling. True, you will still have your share of hard and difficult times, but they are so much easier to get through when you feel good about yourself. You have this incredible optimistic look on things and it is so much easier to pull through the rough times. Believe me, I have been there. Thanks to Spice of Life I have changed my life around and made my life so much more fun to live, and I have finally realized just how happy I can be.

And what a great feeling it is to know I am living my life to its fullest extent and loving each day. Knowing that with each day the happiness and the failures that come with it are molding me for the future. And for me, now I can honestly say that I am coping and I am loving my life.

-- L. Satterlee
Former Spice of Life student

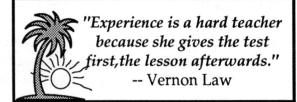

"Experience is a hard teacher because she gives the test first, the lesson afterwards."
-- Vernon Law

Personal Points to Ponder

_____

_____

_____

_____

_____

_____

_____

_____

_____

_____

_____

Personal Points to Ponder

_____

_____

_____

_____

_____

_____

_____

_____

_____

_____

MAINTAINING MOTIVATION

How many times have you heard either from yourself or someone else, "If I were just a bit more motivated to do the things I want to do, I would have no problems at all."

We all have some great ideas, but the real issue is being able to follow through on these great ideas.

. If you do not have a plan to achieve your goals, you are lost.

In this part of *No Negatives* you will explore the art of goal setting and how it can benefit you.

I am sure you have heard the old phrase "Actions speak louder than words." In order for this section to be beneficial to you, action must prevail!

DREAM LIST

In your first step toward achieving the goals you might have set in your mind, let us dream a bit.

I would like for you to complete a short dream list that includes the following areas:

1. Things to Learn:

I would like to learn how to . . .

  a.

  b.

  c.

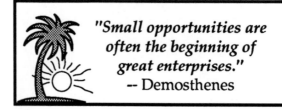

"Small opportunities are often the beginning of great enterprises."
-- Demosthenes

2. Types of People to Meet:

I would like to meet the type of people who are . . .

    a.

    b.

    c.

3. Three Positive Unusual Tasks:

I would like to accomplish . . .

    a.

    b.

    c.

    Now, hold on to these dreams -- you are on your way to turning these dreams to reality.

I THINK
I WOULD BE
GREAT AT

I realize society does not accept our saying in public what we think we are good at, but actually it is a free country and we can do anything (almost) we wish. But then we become the victim of judgmental behavior, and others begin to assume you are "conceited/stuck-up." (Those two words have always been together.) Well, you will now have the opportunity to put down all the things you think you would be great at.

I think I would be great at . . .

1.

2.

3.

4.

5.

6.

7.

8.

9.

10.

Now, hold on to these TOP TEN. They will be beneficial in helping you choose goals.

> *"Procrastination is the art of keeping up with yesterday."*
> -- Don Marquis

GOAL SETTING

Motivation and goal setting go hand in hand. If you are not motivated and organized with a purposeful plan, your goals will have no direction or final outcome.

Here is a story of a man who had lofty goals. He believed, conceived, and captured.

Dr. Daniel Hale Williams, a black man, was born in the mid-1800s in the midst of racial unrest throughout our nation. Because of positive motivation, Dr. Williams applied and was accepted at Northwestern University in 1883. In 1891 he founded Provident Hospital in Chicago, Illinois, where he served as staff surgeon until 1912. He provided training for black interns and nurses, at a time when they had difficulty obtaining medical training in other hospitals, by believing in his goals and following through with his dreams. Dr. Daniel Hale Williams was the first man to successfully complete open heart surgery in 1893.

As young people you often hear from your parents that you should get off your *##!*!! and clean your room. Then if it is not your parents, it is your teachers that want you to be motivated.

Have you ever thought that you would be more motivated if you were better organized, or better yet if someone taught you how to be organized?

That is what it is all about. Next I will identify the three types of goals and you will be on your way.

"Make good habits
and they will
make you."
-- Parks Cousins

IDENTI-FYING GOALS

As mentioned, goals can help you become organized. Goals provide a purpose and direction to your life's activities. A habit of setting a goal for most everything you do should be established, even those more unpleasant activities like cleaning your room and finishing your homework.

In order for goals to work in your favor, one should outline the different levels of goals, those being:

1. Short Range
2. Medium Range
3. Long Range

Short Range Goals are confidence builders. You can reach them in a day, week, or month. Example: keeping your room clean for one week straight. As you begin to set goals, do not be discouraged if you fall short of achieving goals within the time line you have allowed. It takes practice to learn how to adjust for the amount of time needed.

Sample Goal: I will keep my room clean this week.

Medium Range Goals can take anywhere from a few months to a year. For example, if you are taking judo lessons, you master different levels: white, green, brown and black belts. Your green belt might be a medium range goal. As with any goal, achievement requires hard, consistent work. Do not let the length of time needed to reach these goals deter you from trying.

Sample Goal: I will maintain a B average this quarter.

Long Range Goals sometimes scare people. These goals are definitely in the forseeable future, though. In your case a good long range goal could be anywhere from six months to a year.

Sample Goal: I will practice piano four days per week for eight months.

Actually long range goals are the least threatening because you have the most amount of time to accomplish them.

KEY POINTS ON GOAL SETTING

1. **Set goals that will challenge you**. If you are challenged you will be forced to work harder. No pain, no gain!

2. **Set attainable goals.** Be realistic. Almost any goal can be reached, but you must allow for the time it takes to prepare yourself adequately. Goals must be set and achieved in a realistic order. In order to walk, you have got to crawl.

3. **Continue to strive.** After you have achieved some of your goals, continue to set new ones that are even more challenging and rewarding. Do not settle for second best. Remember, you are trying to be the best person you can possibly be. That is achieved by setting higher goals.

4. **Believe in yourself.** Seek out friends and family who will support you. Sometimes goal achievement is a long, tough process. Do not give up. Do not set goals that you hope to achieve -- set goals you *will* achieve.

5. **Set your *own* goals.** Don't be so influenced that you are not doing what *you want to do*.

6. *Expect* **to reach your goals.**

7. **Visualize** your goals. See them happen. (More on this later.)

8. **Make a record** of your goals. (See page 44)

9. **Reevaluate** your goals. Before completing your goals, give them another glance to see if they are within reach. At this point you may need to modify the goals or stretch to achieve them in the time you have set.

10. **Reward** yourself. Plan ahead for celebration. Have it be another positive step ... not something that will undo what you have just accomplished!

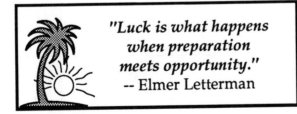

"Luck is what happens when preparation meets opportunity."
-- Elmer Letterman

GOALS

Below, you have been provided with an area designated ofr your short, medium and long range goals. As you can see, the goal charts have been divided into four areas: <u>personal</u>, <u>family</u>, <u>school</u> and <u>other.</u>

As you begin to formulate your goals, use this area as a starting point.

Short Range Goals	**Date Completed**
Personal:	
Family:	
School:	
Other:	

Medium Range Goals

	Date Completed
Personal:	
Family:	
School:	
Other:	

Long Range Goals

	Date Completed
Personal:	
Family:	
School:	
Other:	

OBSTACLES:
PLAN B

Even the best laid plans have the possibility of running wild. Be aware that you may well encounter obstacles in your pursuit of goal achievement. Learn to be flexible and to be able to create other means of achieving what you have set out to do. If you have the ability to develop a "Plan B" you will have better success with goal setting.

Pick a goal that you have set for yourself. Now, take a second to think about some possible obstacles that you may encounter.

    1. List obstacles:

       a.

       b.

       c.

Now, develop an alternative plan that could be used to achieve your goal.

2. Plan B:

a.

b.

c.

This process can be duplicated with any and all of the goals you have set.

Do not allow obstacles to discourage you from pursuing your goals. Everyone encounters barriers from time to time; even some of the most impressive leaders of our country.

Few people remember, but many would be impressed by the track record of one of America's greatest heroes. In 1832 he lost his job and was defeated in a race for the state legislature in 1834. In 1835 a close female companion died, and in 1836 he suffered a nervous breakdown. He lost two more campaigns in 1838 and 1843 before a successful one for Congress in 1846. But he lost his bid for reelection in 1848. He ran for Senate in 1854 and in 1858 and lost both times, and was defeated as a nominee for Vice President in 1856. But everyone remembers that in 1860 Abraham Lincoln was elected President of the United States.

The point should be clear. Mistakes and temporary setbacks hamper everyone. You cannot let yourself worry about making mistakes, and you cannot allow them to get you down after you make them. A temporary setback is far different from utter failure. You do not fail until you accept defeat as permanent and stop trying; that is, you have not failed unless you allow yourself to quit. Instead of despairing because of your mistakes, learn from them.

The method by which we learn best is trial and error. We try, fail, make adjustments, and try again. Few worthwhile achievements -- a great invention, a new theory -- are accomplished in one try; we compensate for our mistakes, "we weed out the bugs" until we succeed. Learn to evaluate your errors and setbacks.

Ask yourself . . .

1. How did I fail?

2. How can I avoid making the same mistake again?

Convert mistakes and setbacks into stepping stones in your progress. Remember, you learn as much from them as you learn from your victories.

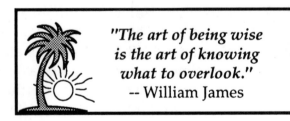

*"The art of being wise
is the art of knowing
what to overlook."*
-- William James

VISUALI-ZATION

Visualization is a process that involves mind over matter. It's the development of images in your mind that will help you to see how to turn a dream into reality. It's almost like a dress rehearsal before a performance. By creating a positive situation in thought, the reality will be easier. Sometimes if you feel you have already done something, to do it again is less difficult. Practice makes perfect.

Goal setting and visualization go hand in hand. Once you have a goal in mind, begin to imagine how, when, why and where you are going to make this goal become a reality.

Visualize by:

1. Putting yourself into a relaxing environment; get comfortable.

2. Pick a goal that you want to visualize.

3. Create a thought process that will enable you to achieve your goal. Ask yourself "Is there a beginning, middle and end in order for your goal to be reached?

4. Make your visualization process as realistic as possible; use as many of your senses as you can.

5. Practice as you awaken, or better yet just before you go to sleep.

MAPPING

Mapping is an activity that requires the use of the visualization process. Basically, mapping is an actual, physical picture of a goal that you want to accomplish. It traces step by step the path you will take toward achievement of your goal. Visualization occurs when you think and see the kinds of things that you will include on your map. Your map will be a kind of collage. A collage is a mixture of pictures and quotes cut from magazines and newspapers. It might also include pictures you have drawn and small items that relate to your goal and have special sentimental value, i.e., ticket stubs, report cards (I didn't say report card, did I?).

Guidelines for making your map:

1. Do a map for a single goal or area on which you are working.

2. Get a good sized piece of cardboard paper.

3. Use lots of color.

4. Include a picture of yourself.

AFFIR-MATION

Occasionally the "I can't" syndrome gets a hold of your thought process. You hit dead ends. You want to give up. In order for this book to work effectively you must become aware of how to fight the "I can't" syndrome.

A simple method called affirmation will help you stay on track so you can successfully accomplish your goals. Affirmation is a process that will help you remove self doubt. To affirm means to make firm. An affirmation is a positive statement that indicates something is already so.

To be good at affirming you must practice -- and then practice some more. By practicing some positive affirmation five to ten minutes daily, I think that you will be surprised with the change in the way you feel about yourself. You'll begin to realize that you are an okay person with enough potential to accomplish what you set your mind to. Also, you will be getting rid of some of those negative concepts you have had about yourself. If you are willing to let it work for you, an affirmation will be one of the best friends you'll ever find.

Below are a few affirmations to help get you started:

1. **The more I commit myself to becoming a better person the more it happens.**

2. **Meeting people is becoming easier for me.**

3. **I can accept people for who they are.**

4. **I am making others happy.**

5. **I am communicating more positively and more freely.**

Key points to remember about affirmations:
1. Phrase affirmations in the present tense, not in the future. Don't say, "I will get along with ____ better." Instead say "I am getting along with ____ better."
2. When using affirmations create a positive feeling within yourself that makes you believe it is actually happening. Don't doubt yourself.
3. Write short, simple affirmations.
4. Place your affirmations on a small 3 x 5 note card and position it in a location where you can be reminded of it, i.e. mirror, purse, wallet, locker, refrigerator, etc.
5. Once you are organized you will be well on your way to making a positive impact on your friends, family, school and community. Use your potential to set goals, and, above all, approach life with this philosophy; If it is to be, it is up to me.

Motivational Questions:

1. If I could travel anywhere in the world, I would go to
   _____. Why?

2. You will receive $25,000.00 if you do a community service project in three months. (Your project must involve 50 people.)

   a. What is your project?

   b. How do you motivate others to do it?

3. In order to receive a passing grade in a class, you must interview three state leaders.

a. Who do you interview? Why?

b. What five questions do you ask them?

1.

2.

3.

4.

5.

Before you go on to Communication, again ask yourself the question, "Have I fully completed this section to the best of my ability?" If yes, proceed; if no, finish it!!

Whenever I hear the word, it does not matter where or what terminology it is used for, I ask myself "What is motivation?" This definition is always running through my mind. Motivation to me is like one of those comic strips; Do you remember that poor, starved man in the desert, begging for water? After crawling for miles does he just give up? NO! He crawls as long as he can. And what about the castaway on the island all alone. Does he give up and jump out of a palm tree? Of course not!

Motivation is something like a line of a poem by an unknown author I once heard:

That within the individual
Which spurs on desire
A desire not fueled by spectators
But a desire fueled by one's self.

Many people have the desire to participate in all of those dreams they had once upon a time. I, like many people, was intimidated by what those so-called "silly expeditions" could lead to. The only thing that is silly about shooting for a dream or goal is not shooting at all -- not taking the risks needed. So I ended up making excuses for not taking an active part in obtaining my dream. Some of my excuses were:

"I cannot. I am too busy." I have learned you are never too busy to take time for yourself! Sometimes you need to make time.

"Why bother. I will just leave it to those who know what they are doing." I was cheating myself out of knowing my own capabilities. This way I would never know.

And how about this one (this has happened to all of us at one time or another). "I will make a fool out of myself. I will never be able to set foot or show my face in this place again!" So what! Swallow all those fears and go for it! Take a risk! To risk means a chance to succeed. Without risk, you will probably be going around in circles with no purpose. Have fun with your dreams. Do whatever you desire to do -- go for it! What is stopping you? The world is your oyster!

As I recall all those times I have needed motivation, one especially comes to mind. My family once lived on 20 acres in the country near Calhan, Colorado. When I was younger, maybe about the age of nine, I would romp through the field pretending I was an Olympian running a marathon. It all was just like a dream. That grass was waist deep and the scent of it is now reminding me of my old home. The sun shone as I strode through the fields. I tumbled down in the grass, and, hiding there in all of its splendor, I would dream of myself as an adult running a foot race.

That summer my dream came true. Mom and Dad had registered me in a two-mile race. I was overjoyed! Mom and I ran the race together, and from that time on I dreamed of being bigger and swifter. As the races became longer, the competition became more fierce. Next was the big three-miler. Boy, was I ready. I had been practicing every day for two weeks.

The day of the race was the day of the butterflies. By that I mean I really had a case of the jitters. Dad told me my butterflies would fly in formation and everything would be peachy.

I had finished stretching out and was checking out all the competition. "Man," I thought, "I am in for it." Everyone was bigger and taller than I was, but it was too late to worry about that. We all lined up to the tape on the asphalt on the course, and the gun went off.

During the race I was keeping up with the girls of the pack, and doing well, too. Nearing the end of the race the girls behind me began passing me. I was pooped and failing fast, but not yet about to give up.

That was when the killer tree attacked. The big oak tree's roots grabbed my foot and sent me sprawling. Although undamaged, I just had to sit down and rest a little, crying soundlessly.

Through squinted eyes I saw a little boy, smaller than me, running like greased lightning through the fresh cut grass alongside the race course. Suddenly I remembered that day that I, in slow motion, had gloriously dashed through the fields near Calhan. "That was it," I said to myself, "here I go." And I was once again dashing through my favorite fields at home.

Of course by then the pack had already finished the race. But I saw the small crowd (in my mind, though, it numbered at least one thousand) cheering and clapping, spurring me on to finish. Across the line I saw my shadow waving to me, urging me to cross the finish line. The feeling of accomplishment was overwhelming!

The bottom line of this story and life is that it does not matter in what place you finish, for motivation is not fueled by spectators, but only by one's self.

-- A. Gillette
Former Spice of Life student

_____

_____

_____

_____

_____

_____

_____

_____

_____

_____

_____

Personal Points to Ponder

_____

_____

_____

_____

_____

_____

_____

_____

_____

_____

_____

COMMUNICATION

Effective communication deals with an area that seldom gets any attention, but it is just as important. That is LISTEN-ING.

If you are an attentive listener, you are probably an effective communicator. If you have problems listening to people and you often interrupt their conversation, then this section of *No Negatives* may be of help.

In this section I will give you some important ideas about effective communication and listening. So sit back, relax, and enjoy.

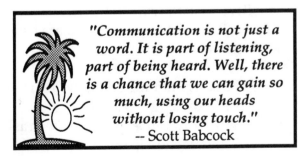

"Communication is not just a word. It is part of listening, part of being heard. Well, there is a chance that we can gain so much, using our heads without losing touch."
-- Scott Babcock

To have the patience, genuine concern, and will to listen is a learned skill. It is nothing special that you are born with, rather a mind set you develop. The following steps are ways to improve your listening skills.

1. **Have the WILL to listen.** People want to be listened to. Do not allow yourself to think someone is not interesting. We all have great stories.
2. **Do not just listen, but COMPREHEND.** Ask yourself if you understood what was being said.
3. **Give POSITIVE CUES** to the person you are listening to. Smile, nod, look them in the eye.
4. **EMPATHIZE with the speaker.** Put yourself in his or her shoes so that you can better understand the speaker's point.
5. **DON'T try to ANTICIPATE** what the speaker is going to say so you can interrupt with an opinion. Hear him/her out.
6. **ASK positive questions.**
7. **DON'T PREJUDGE the person** you are listening to by his/her appearance.

Now that you have a better idea of HOW to listen, let's put this newly acquired knowledge to a test.

As in other areas of *No Negatives* you have been asked to take a risk or two. Well, this section is no different.

1. In a safe situation, go out and meet a stranger. Pick an individual that you know absolutely nothing about. Introduce yourself and spend some time talking to him/ her. You may want to show them this book. Try to make their day more pleasant or let them improve your day.

2. During lunch you notice someone eating alone. Go and join them or ask them to join your group.

3. (Here is a biggie!) There is a particular person you have seldom gotten along with, but you know deep down if you try you can get along with him/her.

4. Create your own situation where you have to take the first step in communication.

HELLO

Not too long ago I heard a story about a lonely and desperate girl. She did not feel as though she quite fit in. She did not have many friends. So one day she decided to go for a walk. She wanted to see how many people would simply greet her with a "Hello." Unfortunately in her pocket was a note that simply stated, "If I can walk from my apartment to the pier and nobody speaks to me, I will jump."

The note was found on her body. Now, I do not know if we can lay the blame on anyone, but it makes you think. <u>You never know how you affect people.</u>

<u>A simple hello never hurts!</u>

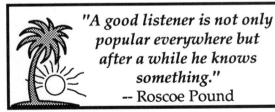

"A good listener is not only popular everywhere but after a while he knows something."
-- Roscoe Pound

**JUST
ASK**

During my first years as a teacher I had the wonderful opportunity to coach basketball and track. During this particular year I was coaching girls basketball and track. Well, it was track season and we had a super team. We won the majority of our meets, with quite a few girls qualifying for the state meet.

One girl in particular had done very well in her first year out for track, finishing third in the 400-meter run. I was so happy for her because it was her first year out. Then I got to wondering why she had not gone out for the team in the previous years. So, I asked her, "Why didn't you compete before?" She looked at me in a very reserved manner and simply stated, *"No one asked me!"*

Needless to say, I learned a good lesson that day. **You never know unless you ask!**

*"We did not all come over
on the same ship, but we
are all in the same boat."* -
- Bernard M. Baruch

J udging: Inevitably judging is something that is common in all of us. I suppose we feel the need to label something good or bad.

The following is a list of suggestions I have compiled to give you some ideas about how to maintain a more positive COMMUNICATION environment.

1. **Try not to prejudge.** Do not judge a book by its cover! If you have ill feelings toward someone or something, get in touch with the real reasons for these feelings. Ask yourself, "Do I feel this way for a GOOD reason or just because I do not like the way that person looks?" We all prejudge at one time or another. Work on minimizing these times.

2. **Do not let others control your actions.** Be yourself! Be in control of your feelings and beliefs.

3. **Find good in others.** Too much time is spent on the negatives.

4. **Practice patience with others.** Make allowances for their differences and weaknesses. No two people are alike. Accept and appreciate.

5. **Learn to like and to understand who or what you might think is undesirable,** i.e. the unpopular, the loner, the sloppy dresser, the plain Jane or Joe. Everyone has something good to offer. Popularity comes and goes. Most people are worth getting to know.

6. **Deal with the facts.** Insensitive moments often result from ignorance. Misunderstandings often occur because someone does not know all the facts.

7. **Listen to your language.** Be aware of what you say. "Hate" is a word often used and overused. Avoid it. "Boring" is just a state of mind that you allow yourself to be a part of.

8. **Empathize.** Begin to put yourself in the other person's shoes. Try to imagine his/her feelings at the time when you might be most critical of him/her.

Now, go out and practice being more sensitive. It is easy!

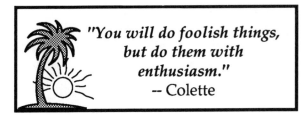

"You will do foolish things, but do them with enthusiasm."
-- Colette

1. You got into a heated discussion with a close friend. You depart not speaking. Later you realize you were wrong. What do you do?

2. You have the opportunity to meet anyone in the world.
   a. Who would it be?

   b. What questions would you ask?

3. What is the biggest risk you have taken involving communication?

4. Who have you (positively) impacted the most in your life?

Before you go on to Community Involvement, ask yourself, "Have I fully completed this section to the best of my ability?" As before, if yes proceed; if no, finish it!!

Here is another testimonial from an alumnus of the Spice of Life program. It truly captures communication for me!

In our world today, communication, whether it be verbal, written or physical, is essential for survival. Communicaton, however, also plays an important role in our relationships with other people. Webster's Collegiate Dictionary defines communication as an exchange of information. But to me communication is much more. I feel it is listening, understanding, and caring. Most of us have had someone come to us with a personal problem at some time or another. Not only may they be seeking advice, but sometimes people just need an ear that is willing to listen. No matter how unimportant the problem may seem, it may go deeper than it appears. I know from personal experience that it can be uncomfortable to have someone confront you with their problems. Being a good listener very often takes strength. However, the results of not listening to an advice-seeker's problem could be devastating.

Studies show that every 90 minutes in America, a young person commits suicide. This does not mean that if you turn away from a friend with a problem he/she will commit suicide. You can never be sure, though, how you will affect others, and five minutes of your time may bring relief and happiness or perhaps even erase the thoughts of suicide from their minds. Spice of Life helped me to listen and communicate with others much more openly and confidently. The day after we discussed listening to others at a Spice of Life meeting, a friend admitted to me that she was thinking of suicide. Although I was scared, I managed to stay calm and discuss the situation with her. My friend is now much happier and receiving professional attention.

Knowing that because I was a good listener I have helped to save a life gives me a good feeling and encourages me to continue to listen to what others have to say. I have also become better at communicating my feelings to others. I realize now that everyone needs someone, and that is okay. To me, it is natural to need someone's shoulder to cry on now and then. Just knowing that someone is there to listen to me makes me a better listener, too.

In my opinion, communication is very important in our lives. Having open lines of communication can make us happier and healthier. And being happy and healthy helps put spice in our lives!

-- A. Speer
Former Spice of Life student

Personal Points to Ponder

_____

_____

_____

_____

_____

_____

_____

_____

_____

_____

Personal Points to Ponder

Personal Points to Ponder

_____

_____

_____

_____

_____

_____

_____

_____

_____

_____

_____

_____

CAREER DEVELOPMENT

by Rich Feller, Ph.D.

Whether it is your first job or one that pays more than the last one, finding a job or deciding what you think you might want to do is a job in itself.

No Negatives wants to help you get a better idea of the type of job you might be interested in as you move through life. And, as throughout the entire *No Negatives* program, we will not just ask you to read, but to DO!

Are you aware of the fact that there are over 30,000 job titles. But if I gave you a sheet of paper and asked you to list as many jobs as you could, how many could you list? Twenty, fifty, a hundred?

O.K., so try it on a separate sheet. List as many jobs as you can right now.

How did you do? Fifty, seventy-five, one hundred fifty? Not bad ... but isn't it amazing to think that there are over 30,000 job titles! If you can only list 50 or so, look at what you could be missing out on. Information is very valuable.

THE INTERVIEW

As you begin to think about what you would like to do for an occupation, I would like to give you a simple activity ... and an opportunity you might find rewarding and informative.

The activity is conducting an interview, actually an informational interview.

All you need to do is identify someone that is in a job you might be interested in. Contact him/her and set up an appointment, at which you will ask the following questions.

1. How did you get this job, or how did you become interested in this kind of work?

2. What do you like/dislike about your work?

3. What would you like to change about your job?

4. In your opinion, what are the problems in your field of work?

5. What are the most important skills you use?

6. How could you be more effective in your job?

7. If you were to change jobs, what would you like to do?

8. Who are two people who do similar work whom I could talk to? May I use your name?

Upon completion of your interview, ask for a business card or their address, and send them a follow-up thank you note.

- Improved attitudes toward work as a valuable part of life and society.

- A better understanding and appreciation of relationships between work and life style patterns.

- Improved ability to communicate with adult workers. A more realistic understanding of how a business organization operates.

- An increased understanding of the private enterprise system. A better understanding of the variety of career paths followed by adult workers during their working life.

- An opportunity to use adult workers as role models for career decision makers.

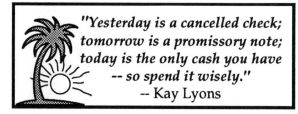

"Yesterday is a cancelled check; tomorrow is a promissory note; today is the only cash you have -- so spend it wisely."
-- Kay Lyons

Personal Points to Ponder

_____

_____

_____

_____

_____

_____

_____

_____

_____

_____

_____

Personal Points to Ponder

_____

_____

_____

_____

_____

_____

_____

_____

_____

_____

_____

HEALTH

It's A Lot More Than Not Being Sick!
by Dr. Tim Houlton

Are you healthy? How do you know? Before we start to look at our state of health, we should define exactly what health is. From Dorlands Medical Dictionary:

> **HEALTH: A state of optimal physical, mental and social well being, and not merely the absence of disease.**

You can see from this definition, that just because you don't have any symptoms of being sick (a stuffy nose, headache, fever...) it doesn't necessarily mean that you're healthy. Health is a state where you're in OPTIMAL SHAPE physically, mentally and socially.

ILLNESS VS. WELLNESS

Have you ever thought about where good health comes from, what causes good health? Let's take an example. If you cut your finger, clean it, put a bandaid on it and wait a few days ... and if you cut a piece of steak, clean it, put a bandaid on it and wait a few days, what's going to happen? Of course your finger will heal, but the steak won't change.

What's the difference? The steak has no life in it, but you are full of life, and THAT is what does the healing. The best doctor you'll ever find is already within your body, ready and willing to heal if you'll provide the right setting for it to happen.

Instead of focusing on what causes illness, let's take some time and look at what causes WELLNESS.

"The doctor of the future will give no medicine but will interest his patients in the care of the human frame, in diet, and in the cause and prevention of disease."
-- Thomas A. Edison

Illness / Wellness Chart

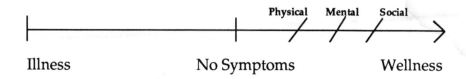

	Physical	Mental	Social

Illness   No Symptoms   Wellness

You should notice a few things about the Illness/Wellness chart. If you are at the point where you have no symptoms of being ill, it doesn't necessarily mean that you are on the wellness end of the chart. As you work on your physical, mental and social well being, you're actually becoming MORE HEALTHY, and helping to PREVENT yourself from becoming sick. There is an arrow on the wellness side of the chart. This shows that as you work on improving your wellness, there's no limit to how great you can feel, and how healthy you can be.

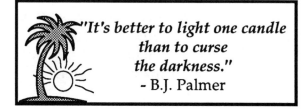

"It's better to light one candle
than to curse
the darkness."
- B.J. Palmer

PHYSICAL WELL BEING

If you wear out your body, where are you going to live? You only have one body, and it has to last you a long time, so it's important to learn earlier, rather than later, how to take care of this wonderful human machine we have.

NUTRITION

If you plant corn, you don't get tomatoes. Likewise if you feed yourself junk food, you're not going to develop a strong, healthy body. The food that you eat and the nutrients that it contains eventually transform to become the tissues of your body, your hair, skin, bones, muscles, blood, nerves ... So you can see that only by eating healthy foods can you develop and maintain a healthy body.

HEALTH TIPS

1. Eat more fresh fruit and vegetables, making sure to eat a variety of types and colors.
2. Eat more whole grain and fiber foods. Examples are whole grain breads, oat bran, brown rice, dried beans, whole bran pasta, fresh vegetables and fruits.
3. Drink 6-8 glasses of water each day. Your body is made up of 80% water, not 80% pop, sodas, diet colas and milkshakes. Natural fruit juices are OK, but cut back on the soft drinks and drink more water.

4. Eat a good breakfast. There's no way you can concentrate properly at school if you haven't had a good breakfast. Yogurt, fruit, whole grain toast, juice, and whole grain cereals with milk are all a great way to start the day.

5. AVOID JUNK FOOD! Remember, you don't want a junk body! Try to limit or avoid totally pop, chocolate bars, candies, cakes, fried foods, fast foods and any foods with preservatives and chemicals. (These will usually be the words on the ingredient label that are hard to pronounce!)

6. Avoid eating too much at one time (overeating), eating when you're upset, when you're not hungry, or late at night.

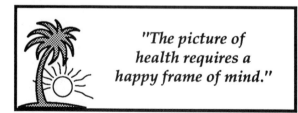

"The picture of health requires a happy frame of mind."

EXERCISE

For the past number of years, there have been very few days that have gone by, where I haven't seen an older man walking down the country road in front of my house. He wears an old fishing cap, and is often carrying some bags.

I stopped to talk with him one day, and found that those bags were grocery bags, and that he walked into town to pick up his groceries. That walk is over ten miles! To me he looked like he was in his sixties, and when I asked him how old he was, he answered, "I'm 84 years young!"

All of us should be so healthy when we're 84! Regular exercise will definitely be one of the most important health tools for you throughout your life.

See if you can list five different types of exercise you want to do.

1.

2.

3.

4.

5.

Regular exercise has many benefits. It's fun, it's challenging, it can be relaxing, it keeps your muscles strong and in good shape, promotes good circulation in your body, keeps your heart and lungs healthy and strong, and helps to prevent many types of illness. Whether it's achieving a new goal in running or swimming, winning or having fun in sports, exercise helps you feel good about yourself, and is something you can do any time, in any season, at any age. It will help you feel good, and look great!

EXERCISE TIPS

1. Exercise at least 3-4 times per week ... NO EXCUSES!

2. Before you exercise, take at least five minutes to stretch and warm up the muscles that you'll be using. It's also a good idea to stretch when you've finished exercising, to help your body cool down.

3. Remember Fashion Show 101? When you exercise, don't be concerned about how you look, how fast or slow you are, winning or losing ... JUST HAVE FUN!

4. IF YOU DON'T USE IT, YOU'LL LOSE IT. If you don't exercise and use the muscles in your body, weakness and poor muscle tone will result. If you have weak muscles, the tendency is to develop bad posture. You

should be very aware of your posture. Sit upright, and don't slump in your school chair. Never carry your books on the same side all of the time, switch arms regularly. Avoid slumping over chairs or curling up on the sofa for hours to watch television. Stay off the sides of your feet when you walk. Also, DO NOT sleep on your stomach. This puts a lot of stress on your neck and lower back. Remember, **as the twig is bent, so grows the tree.** Keep a good posture when you sit, stand and walk ... and even sleep!

Do you realize that every thought and feeling you have directly affects your body? You can't separate the mental and the physical well being ... it is a total health picture. They work together.

Remember the night before your hardest test, or before your biggest game? Your heart was probably beating as fast as it does when you're exercising, but you haven't moved. All of the thoughts and feelings you have effect your body. What's important in determining whether you move towards illness or wellness is your ATTITUDE. It's not what happens to you that counts, it's your attitude in how you handle it.

It is said that attitude creates action, so let's look at the following Attitude Inventory to find negative attitudes which can be switched to more positive attitudes, and move us toward the wellness end of the chart.

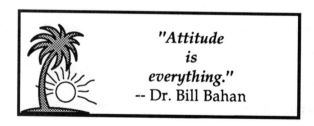

*"Attitude
is
everything."*
-- Dr. Bill Bahan

ATTITUDE INVENTORY

Check the responses that apply to you:

Negative/ Uncreative Attitudes	Positive/ Creative Attitudes
___ My life is full of problems	___ My life is full of challenges
___ Doctors are responsible for my health	___ Doctors may help, but I am responsible for my health
___ Complaining about what you don't have	___ Being thankful for what you do have
___ I have no symptoms, therefore I must be totally healthy	___ I can always improve my health by working on my physical, mental & social well being
___ I know how other people should behave	___ I accept other people for who they are
___ I look for the negative in every situation	___ I look for the positive in every situation
___ It's all a matter of luck	___ I get back what I put out
___ I'm afraid to do it	___ I'll do my best and go for it, regardless of the outcome
___ The glass is half empty	___ The glass is half full
___ That's not funny!	___ I never forget a sense of humor

I will make the following changes in my diet:

1.

2.

3.

4.

5.

The changes I would like to make in my exercise schedule and new activites I would like to try are:

1.

2.

3.

4.

5.

Take your own personal Attitude Inventory. What are some of the attitudes you have, which you would like to change?

Negative/ Uncreative Attitudes	Positive/ Creative Attitudes

Hopefully, you've learned a bit more about health and wellness, but remember ... **KNOWLEDGE IS THE POWER, BUT ENTHUSIASM THROWS THE SWITCH.** Be enthusiastic about improving your health. Take care of your body, but also take care of your thoughts and feelings, your attitudes, and your relationships with others. Not only will you feel better and have less symptoms of illness, but you'll experience a new HIGH LEVEL OF WELLNESS. Have fun!

"If it is to be, it's up to me."
-- unknown

Personal Points to Ponder

_____

_____

_____

_____

_____

_____

_____

_____

_____

_____

_____

_____

Personal Points to Ponder

_____

_____

_____

_____

_____

_____

_____

_____

_____

_____

_____

Personal Points to Ponder

_____

_____

_____

_____

_____

_____

_____

_____

_____

_____

_____

LITERACY

by Robert T. Williams, Ed.D.

Literacy is having the reading, writing, speaking, listening, computing, and problem solving skills to be able to take advantage of the quality of life available to you. This includes both your academic and personal life.

In your academic life, being literate includes being able to read, write, speak, compute and problem solve, so that you can take advantage of the quality of life available to you in your classes. This means that you are becoming literate in literature, mathematics, economics, agriculture, physical education, music, art, home economics, business finance, and other courses you are taking in school.

To develop your academic literacy skills, you will want to attend to the study skills and learning suggestions your teacher gives to you. Your teacher is an expert learner in their content area. They have developed their literacy skills in that area. They can help you become literate in that content area too. So if you are having trouble ask your teacher to help you with your class literacy.

Also, you may want to take a general study skills or reading improvement course. These courses will help you develop the general literacy skills which are useful in almost all of your classes.

Another suggestion to improve your literacy skills is to ask a successful student for help. Ask them how they learn, how they study, how they problem solve in class.

You also will want to develop your personal literacy skills. These skills include being able to fill out job applications, balance your bank account, follow directions in completing projects, reading street signs and road maps, reading medicine labels, understanding credit agreements, reading advertisements, and other skills needed for functioning in your daily life.

Many of these personal literacy skills are called "survival" literacy skills, because they are needed to survive in society today. Many people make their living providing literacy skills for other people. For example, accountants and tax experts help people less literate to prepare their income taxes each year. Also, lawyers read and write for people who do not know how and do not want to take the time to read and write their own agreements.

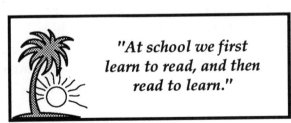

"At school we first learn to read, and then read to learn."

You can become more personally literate by asking your parents, or another person who will serve as a mentor to you (you may want to get several mentors to help you with all of the literacy skills you will want to learn) about how to read and understand certain information, how to understand when you hear information, and how to speak about that information. There are also booklets available through the federal government and your local extension agent which will give you tips to increase your literacy.

Other people need assistance in increasing their literacy skills, too. Some of these people are young children, some are in school, and some are adults. You can help others increase their literacy skills!

You could volunteer to read to young children, either through the schools or through your local library. Reading to children is very important in helping those children learn to read. They are not trying to read yet, but being read to is one of the best ways to help them get ready to read.

If you are good in a subject, that is you have well developed literacy skills, you might want to help someone else become more literate in that area. This will help solidify your skills, too. So, ask your teacher or counselor if you could become a peer tutor.

There are community efforts to assist adults who lack literacy skills. You can volunteer through your local literacy agency or library. There will be training to assist you in helping others.

Also, you could contact your local university, or the adult

education/literacy section of the Department of Education in your state. When you are in post-secondary school you will want to become involved with the Student Literacy Corps on your campus. The SLC is a program funded by the United States Department of Education. It establishes a course or courses in community colleges and university campuses which educate undergraduate students in becoming tutors of adults who lack literacy skills. The course(s) require that you tutor an adult while you are taking classes. You learn and practice at the same time. Everybody learns!

So, becoming literate is being able to take advantage of the quality of life available to you. There is a fine quality of life if you have the literacy skills. There is a lesser quality of life with each literacy skill you lack.

Commit yourself to becoming literate and proficient in your academic and personal pursuits. Few people are "dumb," but many people lack literacy skills. If you lack literacy skills, go find out how to get them. If somebody needs a literacy skill that you have, help them obtain it.

Increasing your literacy skills, or helping someone increase theirs, will boost your self confidence. It's all part of being the best you can be.

"Those who don't read good books have no advantage over those who can't read them."

As you begin to develop a plan for HOW you are going to implement literacy into your daily life, ask yourself the four W's: WHAT specifically are you going to do, WHO will be involved with your literacy assignment, WHEN will it take place, and WHERE will it be?

What:

Who:

When:

Where:

Good Luck!

Personal Points to Ponder

_____

_____

_____

_____

_____

_____

_____

_____

_____

_____

_____

Personal Points to Ponder

_____

_____

_____

_____

_____

_____

_____

_____

_____

_____

_____

Personal Points to Ponder

_____

_____

_____

_____

_____

_____

_____

_____

_____

_____

_____

TIME MANAGEMENT

by Jill Noel

How many times have you heard your parents, teachers, or others: "You are wasting your time!" You probably ask yourself, "What difference does it make what I do with my time?" Hopefully, after reading this section on time management, you will have a good feel for the importance of managing your time.

We need to ask ourselves, what value is there in managing our time? After all, isn't time something that we will always have?

Managing our time wisely allows us to do three things:
1. Accomplish the tasks that we NEED to get done (i.e. go to school, finish papers, eat, sleep, clean room, etc.)
2. Have time to the things we WANT to do (i.e. go to a movie with friends, play sports, go to dances, read, shop, etc.)
3. Use time to plan ahead for the future (i.e. where you might want to go to college, where you can go on vacation, what you might buy for a friend's birthday, etc.)

Let's explore how well you manage your time. Ask yourself the following questions:

Do you ever analyze your daily routine to see where your time goes? _____ Yes _____ No

Do you have a system for keeping track of daily "things to do?" _____ Yes _____ No

Do you do your most important jobs first? _____ Yes _____ No

Do you use a weekly schedule? _____ Yes _____ No

Do you schedule time each day for rest, relaxation and physical activity? _____ Yes _____ No

How did you do? Are you organized with your time and the tasks you need to do? If not, there is a way you can help yourself! It's quick and easy and will give you a sense of accomplishment at the end of your day. Try it! You'll like it!

If you don't have time to do it right, when will you have time to do it over?

"TO DO" LIST

Make a DAILY "To Do" list.

I Must Do	I Should Do	I Could Do
1.		
2.		
3.		
4.		

DO IT NOW! Procrastination only lends itself to frustration and devastation!

Now that you have a good grasp of how to prioritize the things you need to accomplish, let's look at the different strategies you can adopt to help you change your time management habits:

- Don't try to do everything at once
- Get someone else to help you -- SUPPORT HELPS!
- Don't get down on yourself if you slip up
- Reward yourself for the changes and progress you *do* make

Remember, improvements in your time management skills are things only *you* are likely to see!

<u>DANGER</u>: Following the above set of guidelines may be hazardous to your health!! It may result in more organized, smooth-sailing, fun-filled days!!

"Some people count time, others make time count."

TIME MANAGEMENT TIPS

As you can see, managing your time can be fun and creative! If you dedicate time each morning to plan your daily tasks, you will find yourself saving time in the long run! It is a fact that more time is wasted by not being organized than by taking the initial time to plan your work! In order to stay organized, use these time management tips to help you stay on track:

1. Keep an appointment book or a spiral notebook
2. Write a "to do" list every day
3. Make the most of every spare minute
4. Make the most of transition times
5. Learn to say NO when appropriate (Make sure you have enough time for yourself.)
6. Control interruptions
7. Wean yourself from the television
8. Concentrate on one thing at a time
9. Develop procedures for routine matters
10. Spend more time in planning (Challenge yourself to write things down, don't just think about it.)
11. Ask the question "What is the best use of my time right now?"
12. Don't be afraid to make mistakes (We learn very important lessons from our mistakes.)

13. Break tasks down into 15-30 minute intervals so you can utilize the little times in your day
14. Don't spend any more time sleeping than what is needed
15. Run as many errands as possible at one time
16. Don't spread yourself too thin!
17. BUILD YOUR WILL POWER -- time management is self-discipline!

Starting NOW to manage your time will teach you good habits for the future! Some of the most successful people in this world are ones who have mastered the art of time management. IT PAYS TO PLAN!

Good Luck! YOU CAN DO IT!!

> *"Time changes with time: in youth, time marches on; in middle age time flies; and in old age, time runs out. Manage your time!"*

Personal Points to Ponder

_____

_____

_____

_____

_____

_____

_____

_____

_____

_____

_____

Personal Points to Ponder

_____

_____

_____

_____

_____

_____

_____

_____

_____

_____

_____

COMMUNITY SERVICE

In 1980 I had a most unique opportunity. I was selected to travel with the international, educational organization Up With People.

For those of you unfamiliar with Up With People, this is a non-profit educational organization whose primary goal is to build bridges of communication and understanding between all cultures of the world through a two-hour musical performance and community service efforts.

After a year of traveling to over eighty different cities throughout the United States and Europe, the one aspect that still plays an important role in my life today is the emphasis on community service projects. Both individually and with students I have worked on projects ranging from working in community soup kitchens, to spending a day with a senior citizen and volunteering at the Special Olympics.

With each and every opportunity I found a greater sense of concern for each project I got involved with. I found myself saying "I wish I would have been doing this when I was younger," but I realized that it's never too late to start anything!

So, what can I do, you might ask. Believe it or not, we all have a skill at something. It might be listening, working with animals, writing, teaching, typing, storytelling, tree planting, baking, organizing, office work, photography, computer work, or what have you.

As you plan to get involved with the community, you may want to ask the following questions:

1a. What population do I want to work with (young, old, homeless, physically or mentally challenged)?

1b. Focus Area:_____

2a. How much time do I want to invest per week?

2b. Time:_____

3a. In exactly what area do I want to focus (social issues, i.e. soup kitchen; or service, i.e. day care)?

3b. Area:_____

"When you give, we all get."

Now that you have narrowed down your choice of where you would like to do your community service project, your next step will center around finding an organization. Your community may have a United Way agency that can give you a list of resources.

Upon careful investigation of this list, pick two or three organizations that may be of interest to you. After you have done that, call and set up an appointment for a site visit.

After your site visit you will have a good feel for the agency that is best for you. Once that happens you are on your way to becoming an active citizen in and of your community.

*"We make a living
by what we get,
but we make a life
by what we give."*

Think you are done, right? Well, there is one more step. That step is processing!

Ask yourself the following questions:

1. What have I accomplished?

2. Did my experience meet my expectations?

3. What would I do differently?

4. Why was this important to me?

5. Could I have given more of myself?

6. What did I gain?

7. How can I apply this to daily life?

Now you are complete. Remember, the more you give of yourself in an unconditional way, the better you will feel about yourself.

Now take these tools and tell a friend.

Personal Points to Ponder

_____

_____

_____

_____

_____

_____

_____

_____

_____

_____

_____

Personal Points to Ponder

_____

_____

_____

_____

_____

_____

_____

_____

_____

_____

_____

MENTORING

Imagine having an older friend who you would spend time with once a week, twice a month, that has all the wisdom and experience in life you WISHED you possessed.

That scenario is not out of your reach. How, you might ask? By finding a mentor.

What is a mentor? A mentor is a person who oversees the development and leadership path, through teaching, counseling, listening and providing overall support, to the mentee (that's you!). Mentoring is also a structured, enduring relationship between a young person and an adult, who provides help, support and guidance. The aim of mentoring is to develop in the young person the skills and self confidence necessary for a fulfilling life.

Sound like something you would be interested in? If so, read on!

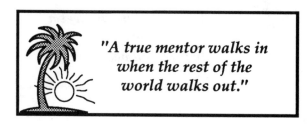

"A true mentor walks in when the rest of the world walks out."

Next, we will look at the following two questions: 'What will a good mentor do for me?' and 'How can I find a mentor?'

A good mentor is a role model, friend, or teacher who...

... supports, encourages and guides you.

... helps you build your self esteem.

... listens carefully for feelings as well as content.

... shares your aspirations and dreams.

... helps you design realistic goals.

... provides opportunities that fit your needs.

... shows you how to be independent and responsible.

... is a good motivator.

... above all, **BELIEVES IN YOU!**

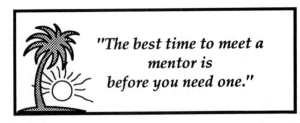

"The best time to meet a mentor is before you need one."

How can you find a mentor? That's easy – just ask! Go over the list on the previous page, and become familiar with what a mentor can do for you. You will need to narrow down the list to fit you. Don't be put off if you think you don't know someone with these qualities. They are out there! Ask your parents to help.

Also, you might consider the following types of people as a mentor:

- Doctor
- Lawyer
- Teacher
- College Professor
- Nurse
- Entrepreneurs (look it up!)
- City Employees (Mayor, police, etc.)
- Performer
- or anyone else you respect and admire

After you locate this individual you might find useful a discussion about:
- work, school or home adjustment
- educational or career goals
- ways to communicate more effectively with friends and family
- the mentor's place of employment (maybe spend a day with him/her)

Or go together to a movie, skiing, bike riding, shopping, to dinner with his or her family, or just sit and talk. These will be opportunities to get to know each other better.

As you can see, the choices are wide open. Don't limit yourself to the amount of fun you can have!

Finally, a few responsibilities of the mentee (that's you!):

1. **You should be time-conscious.** <u>Keep all appointments you set with your mentor.</u> If an appointment has to be cancelled, the mentor should be contacted. If a mentor cannot be reached on the phone, a message should be left.

2. **A mentee should initiate meeting** with his/her mentor. Even though a mentee is a student, a lot of the responsibility for success of the relationship depends on the mentee.

So, go out and make somebody's day by asking them to be *your* mentor! They will be honored.

(Resource: Colorado State's Minority Mentoring Program)

"A true mentor will see you through when others see that you are through."

Personal Points to Ponder

_____

_____

_____

_____

_____

_____

_____

_____

_____

_____

_____

Personal Points to Ponder

SUMMARY

Now that you have successfully completed *No Negatives*, go and celebrate, and make someone's day.

As you continue to move through life you will have many opportunities to utilize these *No Negative* principles daily. I urge you to do so in the most positive and productive way you choose.

If your school or community is interested in having J. Victor McGuire for a No Negatives Seminar, or to order additional *No Negatives* books, please write to Spice of Life at the address below.

Also, we would welcome stories or experiences that relate to *No Negatives*. Please send your letters to:

Spice of Life
111 E. Drake Road, #7065
Fort Collins, CO 80525

> Best of Luck,
> J. Victor McGuire

REMEMBER...

*Whatever your mind can
conceive and believe,
it will achieve.*

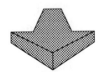

*Just don't look back
unless you want to go that way.*

You are unique.
In all the history of the world
there was never anyone else
exactly like you.
And in all the infinity to come
there will never be
another you.

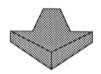

For every obstacle
there is a solution.

*Nothing in the world
can take the place
of persistence.*

*Do
it
now.*

*There is no failure
except in
no longer trying.*

*You can always
better your best.*

To accomplish great things,
you must not only act,
but also dream;
not only plan,
but also believe.

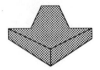

The greatest mistake
is giving up.

*If you have built
castles in the air,
you need not be lost --
put foundations under them.*

*Success is an attitude.
Get yours right!*

SUGGESTED READING LIST

The Way of the Peaceful Warrior, by Dan Millman

The Tao of Leadership, by John Heider

Hope for the Flowers, by Trina Paulus

Castle of the Pearl, by Christopher Biffle

The Way of the Bull, by Leo Buscaglia

If You Don't Know Where You're Going You'll Probably End Up Somewhere Else, by David Campbell

All Grown Up & No Place To Go: Teenagers in Crisis, by David Elkind

Creative Visualization, by Shakti Gawain

The Hug Therapy Book, by Kathleen Keating

The Giving Tree, and *Missing Piece,* by Shel Silverstein

Velveteen Rabbit,, by Margery Williams

Go For It, by Judy Zerafa

NO NEGATIVES
T-SHIRT & BOOK ORDER FORM

(Photocopy this order form as necessary)

T-shirt is 50% Cotton/ 50% Polyester, with a red and black design

Qty	Item	Size S, M, L, XL	Price Ea.	Total
	No Negatives T-Shirt		11.95	
	No Negatives Book		12.95	
		SUBTOTAL		
	Colo. residents add 5.75% TAX			
	Add 15% for SHIPPING			
		TOTAL		

Name _____

Address _____

City/State/Zip _____

Phone (   ) _____

Make check payable to Spice of Life and mail to:

Spice of Life
111 E. Drake Rd., #7065
Fort Collins, CO 80525

Discounts available on book orders of 30 or more.
Allow 3 weeks for delivery.